Iain Heggie

# King of Scotland

*and*

# The Tobacco Merchant's Lawyer

T0258367

**Methuen Drama**

Published by Methuen Drama 2011

Methuen Drama, an imprint of Bloomsbury Publishing Plc

1 3 5 7 9 10 8 6 4 2

Methuen Drama
Bloomsbury Publishing Plc
36 Soho Square
London W1D 3QY
www.methuendrama.com

*King of Scotland* and *The Tobacco Merchant's Lawyer*
first published by Methuen Drama in 2011

Copyright © 2011 Iain Heggie

Iain Heggie has asserted his rights under the Copyright, Designs
and Patents Act 1988 to be identified as the author of this work

ISBN: 978 1 408 15644 5

Available in the USA from Bloomsbury Academic & Professional,
175 Fifth Avenue/3rd Floor, New York, NY 10010.
www.BloomsburyAcademicUSA.com

A CIP catalogue record for this book is available from
the British Library

Typeset by Country Setting, Kingsdown, Kent

GLASGOW ACTORS

*in association with*
The Tron Theatre
*present*

# King of Scotland

## by Iain Heggie

**TRON**
**THEATRE**

# King of Scotland

## by Iain Heggie

Tommy McMillan    Jonathan Watson

| | |
|---|---|
| Director | Iain Heggie |
| Production Manager | Woody McMillan |
| Designer | Peter Screen |
| Lighting Designer | Andrew Wilson |
| Tour Booker | Kirsty Shea |
| Produced by | Jonathan Watson and Iain Heggie |
| Poster by | John Cairns |
| Poster Photography | Bob Balmer |
| Show photography | Mike Brooke |

With thanks to RSAMD, Tron Theatre
and Liz Carruthers

Artistic policy: see page vii

# Cast and Creatives

## Jonathan Watson

Born in Glasgow, Jonathan trained at the Royal Scottish Academy of Music and Drama. On leaving college he joined the Glasgow Citizens' T.A.G. Theatre Company and went on to work with the Traverse, Borderline, 7:84, Royal Lyceum, Perth Rep., and the Scottish Theatre Co., while returning to the Citizens on many occasions.

While featuring in several television dramas earlier on in his career, it was his association with BBC Scotland's Comedy Unit that brought him to the public's attention. *Naked Video, City Lights*, and *Rab C. Nesbitt* are just some of the programmes he has been involved in.

However, it is the satirical look at Scottish football – seen through the eyes of *Only An Excuse?* – for which he is best known. Transmitted just before the bells, BBC Scotland's *Only an Excuse? Hogmanay Special* attracts an audience of over a million viewers each year. The show has also enjoyed great success when transferred to the stage.

In April, Jonathan appeared at the Magners International Comedy Festival with a stage version of his long running radio show *Watson's Wind Up Live!*, playing to a sell-out crowd at the Citizens' Theatre.

This year sees Jonathan returning to the theatre in Iain Heggie's *King of Scotland* at The Tron, then touring, before taking the production to the Edinburgh Fringe Festival.

Film work includes: *Local Hero, Girl in the Picture, The Match* and *Solid Geometry*.

Television work also includes, *The Bill, Casualty*, the award-winning *New Town* and *Garrow's Law*.

Jonathan has recently completed filming an episode of BBC'S *New Tricks*.

## Iain Heggie

is the writer of the recent *The Tobacco Merchants Lawyer*, which received EIGHT four-star reviews, and the award-winning *Wholly Healthy Glasgow, American Bagpipes*, and *Wiping My Mother's Arse*. Other theatre work includes *The Sex Comedies, Politics in the Park, Lust, An Experienced Woman Gives Advice, The Don* and preliminary versions of *Sauchiehall Street* and *Global Warming Is Gay*.

Radio credits include *Zeitgeist Man, The Actor's Agent's Tale* and *Funeral Catering in the 21st Century*. He is under commission to the National Theatre of Scotland and Oran Mor.

Previous directing work at the Tron: *Beauty Queen of Leenane, Hollywood*, and a preliminary version of *Like This* by Julie Tsang.

Having trained to act and sing, he has started performing again in cabaret in the last few years, writing his own monologues and song lyrics. This gave rise to a try-out one man show *Wide Asleep* at The Tron and the Finborough, London in 2009. This has now given birth to two fully-fledged one-man shows: *People I Tried to Like* and *Love Songs for a Timewaster* (music by Christine Bovill, John Kielty and Tyler Collins). Both will be premiered at the Gilded Balloon in this year's fringe.

### Peter Screen

studied at the RSAMD and graduated with a BA Stage Management Studies in 2001. Design credits include *Project Branded, Fallen, Samurai* and many more for Tron Participation. At present he is Director for Upstage Theatre Productions and his designs include, *Steel Magnolias, Musical of Musicals, Calamity Jane, Stepping Out, The Wiz, The Steamie* and many more. At present he can be found as Front of House and Events Manager for the Tron Theatre.

### Andrew Wilson

has worked as a lighting designer for many years – on productions of all sizes from the tiniest theatre in the land to the largest stage in Europe. Recent credits include: *Gagarin Way* for Rapture Theatre (UK Tour), *The Lasses, O* and *The Ragged Lion* for Rowantree Theatre (Scottish Tours), *Lanza* for Cast Theatre (UK Tour), *Love's Time's Beggar* for Ankur Productions, *Fugee* and *Blackout* for RSAMD Dramaworks, *The Emotional Life of Furniture* for Spartan Productions and *Beating the Drum for Africa* for the Usher Hall.

### Woody McMillan

has been working in technical theatre and concert lighting in the UK since 1990. He recently did the lighting design for Julie Tsang's sell-out first play *Like This* . . . at the Tron.

### Kirsty Shea

was a stage manager for nine years, working for various companies such as Brunton Theatre Company, the Royal Lyceum, Traverse Theatre, Tron Theatre, 7:84 Theatre Company and various other touring theatre companies. For the past five years Kirsty has been working as the Assistant to the Directors at the Tron Theatre as well as occasionally company managing for smaller Scottish Theatre Companies.

# Tour Schedule 2011

| | |
|---|---|
| Lemon Tree, Aberdeen | Wed 18 May |
| Howden Park, Livingston | Fri 20 May |
| Byre, St Andrews | Sat 21 May |
| Macrobert, Stirling | Wed 25 May |
| Eden Court, Inverness | Fri 27, Sat 28 May |
| Harbour Arts, Irvine | Thurs 2 June |
| Arts Guild, Greenock | Fri 3 June |
| Carnegie Hall, Dunfermline | Sat 4 June |

Assembly at the Assembly Halls
on The Mound, Edinburgh,
and throughout the fringe in August

## Glasgow Actors

Glasgow Actors was set up in 2011.
*King of Scotland* is their second production.

Artistic policy: artistic policy my arse!

# Forthcoming Shows by Iain Heggie

## PEOPLE I TRIED TO LIKE

Gilded Balloon at the Edinburgh Fringe
229 August, 2.00 pm

If the people in your life are like the people in Iain Heggie's, could you cope? There's 96-year-old Granny Bain, the confused sectarian who thinks the Queen is a Catholic; neighbour Ann Marie, the suicidal 6'3" trans-sexual; and the politically correct cousin Campbell, whose wife Fatima was selected from an ethnic minority short-list. Iain Heggie tried to like his friends, neighbours and relatives. Could you do any better?

Razor-sharp and hilarious. Written by and starring the writer of *King of Scotland* and *The Tobacco Merchant's Lawyer*.

## LOVE SONGS FOR A TIMEWASTER

Gilded Balloon at the Edinburgh Fringe
18–29 August, 6.45 pm

'I wouldn't go out with anyone that went out with me.' This
unique combination of song, comedy and drama explores love
from an adult point of view. We know nobody is perfect, but
how much imperfection should you put up with? Hilarious,
touching and inspiring, this is a route map for how to fall out of
love with a person and fall in love with life. A one-man musical,
with the writer and friends.

'Beautiful, funny, thoughtful lyrics.' Iain Heggie's voice is full of
edge and tension' (*Scotsman*).

# King of Scotland

Freely adapted from the short story
'Diary of a Madman' by Gogol

**Character**

**Tommy McMillan**

## Scene One

**Tommy**'s *bedroom in his multi-storey home.*

*Bed with TV at the foot of it, table and chair, coat stand, a door. Possibly a window.*

*We find* **Tommy** *searching. He is not wearing jacket or shoes. He finds random object. He throws it away. He sees us.*

### 1.

I'd've even been happy with a budgie.

But they're like: 'No pets allowed in these flats.'

I'm like: 'Be nice.

A wee pet.

Be company.'

They're like: 'That's the rules.'

I'm like: 'Aw, fuck the rules.'

They're like: 'Do you want the flat or not?'

I'm like: 'Nice of you to offer.

I know they're in demand.'

They're like: 'Are you joking?

No one wants them.

They're classified hard to let.'

I'm like: 'Perfect.

I'll take it.

If they're hard to let that'll discourage the riffraff.'

Move in.

Turns out the entire building's teeming.

And not just with the riffraff.

Also their pets.

Dogs, cats, canaries, hamsters, a snake.

It's like a zoo in these flats.

Which is a complete scandal.

Totally contrary to the rules.

And the noise is diabolical.

I'm going deaf with the racket.

So no way am I getting a budgie.

Tweet, tweet, tweet.

I'd end up ringing the noisy wee bam's neck.

Oh, I'd've arranged a funeral.

Minister in.

Cup of tea all round.

Budgies are human too.

**Tommy** *continues searching. He finds another random object, which he throws away.*


## 2.

Which is more than I can say for some people.

That government of ours.

OK the unemployment levels are on the climb.

But sending people for interviews?

To train for work.

In a call centre.

At the Department of Social Inclusion.

In among all the bams and scum.

And if folk are no wantin' to work?

Makin' them work anyway!

So it's compassion down the shithole with this government.

They don't seem to realise it's a lifetime achievement:

Twenty-eight consecutive years of unemployment.

But I'm a fighter.

I'll show them.

All my life I've been good for nothing.

And I'm not changing now.

**Tommy** *searches, finds a cup of tea. He goes to throw it away. He changes his mind and drinks.*

**3.**

So I'm sitting in this interview.

This Sir Alec guy.

Posh cunt.

You know the type.

*Burke's Peerages* coming out his arse.

My kind of guy, you know?

He's like: 'And tell me Tommy, how long have you been unemployed?'

I'm like: 'Twenty-eight years, Sir Alec.'

He's like: 'That's it.

Interview over.

Sorry it was so short.'

I'm like: 'What have I done wrong?'

He's like: 'Nothing.

You've done nothing wrong.

You're exactly what we're looking for.

When can you start?'

So good on Sir Alec.

He's seen the future.

So he has.

And I'm it.

Oh, you hear all the wankstains.

They're all calling him Sir Smartaleck.

Behind his back.

Which is like totally unfair.

The guy actually deserves a medal.

He's struggling by on three-hundred-and-odd grand a year.

When it's an established fact posh cunts like him need to clear at least a million.

They've got estates the size of Africa to maintain.

**Tommy** *puts down his tea, goes to search and rapidly interrupts himself.*


**4.**

Job sucks though.

Well, no wonder.

It's that Nicola.

Specs, big honk, hairy ears.

How are you supposed to respect the nebby cow?

Total schemie.

But thinks she can tell me what to do.

Just because she's above me at work.

Sink estate, the slag.

Sink estate and the cheek to stay on for her highers!

Gets in to the department.

Pushes shoves sucks cock till she gets floor supervisor.

She's not well liked.

**Tommy** *searches He finds a shoe puts it on.*


### 5.

As for all the other bams in the work.

Seeking asylum seemingly – half of them.

I say to them – (*Loud voice.*) 'If it's an asylum you're seeking you're in the wrong place.

The asylum's in Edinburgh.

It's the shite modern building at the bottom of the hill.

Just keep away from the ancient wan at the top but.

That's not for the likes of youse.'

Wouldny mind.

But they don't even bother to learn the lingo.

Canny understand a word they're sayin'.

Guarantee every word they speak'll be utter gibberish.

Which is actually my favourite language.

And ideas above their station.

These asylum seekers.

Well, one shag a month and think they're God.

That's only one shag more than I get.


**6.**

Then the big man himself.

The Minister for Social Inclusion.

Big Danny.

Workaholic seemingly.

False reputation if you ask me.

Never see the prick.

Nicola's like:

'He works in London.'

I'm like:

'What's the point of him working in London?

Everybody in London's already included.

Should be working up here.

Up here everybody's all still excluded.'

Lackadaisical cunt.

**Tommy** *searches, hobbling on one foot. He gives up.*


**7.**

This work malarkey definitely does suck but.

If it wasn't for Sir Alec I'd be out.

Few weeks ago there.

Nicola's like: 'I'm fed up with you.

Go and see Sir Alec.

He's in his office.'

He's like: 'How are you getting on, Tommy?'

I'm like: 'To tell you the truth, Sir Alec, I'm thinking of chucking it.'

He's like: 'What's wrong?'

I'm like: 'Well it's one scumbag on the phone after another.

And they're giving it: "I'm socially excluded.

I want my rights."

So I'll be like: "Sorry, Jim.

I can't help you."

So they'll be like: "That's a disgrace.

The entire point of your department is to fight social exclusion."

So I'll be like: "Correction.

The entire point of this department is to keep the likes of me included.

And the likes of you excluded."'

Then Sir Alec's like: 'I think you better come and work in my office.'

I'm like: 'What do you want me to do?'

He's like: 'Nothing.'

I'm like: 'Nothing?'

He's like: 'Between you and me, nothing at all.'

I'm like: 'Nothing at all?'

He's like: 'I think we both know you have a special talent for it.'

Nice to be appreciated for once in my life.

Then he's like: 'I particularly want you to meet the Minister.

Yes, next time he's here I'll introduce you.

Big Danny will love you.'

*He resumes searching. Gives up.*


**8.**

Lying in my bed this morning.

I'm like: 'Will I go to my work?

Will I not go to my work?'

In comes big fat Jackie.

Brings me in my tea.

Puts it down.

Says nothing.

I say nothing.

She heads back out.

As usual.

The bad manners of her is unbelievable.

Shout her back in.

I'm like: 'You got the time?'

She's like: 'It's pushing nine, Tommy.'

I'm like: 'It is not.'

She's like: 'It is so.'

I'm like: 'You might have said.'

She's like: 'That's what I just did.'

Totally argumentative, big fat Jackie.

It's a result of her being scum.

You try not to rub it in.


**9.**

In to work.

Wish I hadn't bothered.

Sir Alec's not in.

His office door's locked.

I'm hanging about the department floor.

Trying to help out.

Up comes nebby Nicola with the hairy ears.

Face on her like soiled toilet paper.

She's like: 'What are you on, Tommy?'

I'm like: 'I'm on fuck all, Nicola.'

She's like: 'You're going about like a bam.'

I'm like: 'I'm are not.'

She's like: 'You're going up to people's screens and typing in obscenities.'

I'm like: 'I'm typing in the truth.'

She's like: ' "All schemie slags suck cock", is the truth?'

I'm like: 'Have I not spelt it right?'

She's like: 'You can't get away with this.'

I'm like: 'Oh, but I can.'

She's like: 'I'll have to talk to Sir Alec.'

I'm like: 'Where is he?'

She's like: 'Edinburgh still.'

I'm like: 'When's he coming back?'

She's like: 'I haven't the faintest idea.'

But she's wasting her time, the slag.

Sir Alec and me are like that.

We buy each another Christmas cards.

**Tommy** *goes to coat stand. Goes to take jacket off and interrupts himself.*


## 10.

But I thought: 'Fuck it.

Sir Alec's in Edinburgh.

I'll take the afternoon off.'

Home.

Just in and big fat Jackie's giving it:

'What you doing home, Tommy?'

I'm like: 'Sir Alec gave me the afternoon off.'

She's like: 'There's mould under the kitchen window again.

Could you go and see the Housing Association?'

I'm like: 'Could you not go?'

She's like: 'My bronchitis is back.'

I'm like: 'Och Jackie.'

She's like: 'Never mind och Jackie.

Get out and do it.'

Know something about Jackie?

Doesn't realise who she's talking to.

*He takes his jacket from the coat stand, puts the jacket over his arm. Another shoe is on the hook under the jacket. He sees this, and takes the shoe down. He looks at it for a second and then hobbles out, still wearing one shoe with the jacket on one arm and the new shoe held in the opposite hand.*

## Scene Two

*Dinner is on the table with cutlery. The food is not visible, under a cloche-type cover.*

### 1.

**Tommy** *comes in wearing his coat, now with both shoes on. He goes to the coat stand and starts taking his coat off. Suddenly, with the coat half off, he stops half way and turns to us.*

See me.

Basically I'm a dog person.

Should've got one years ago.

Every bit as good as people.

If not better.

They can do a lot we can't do.

They're not embarrassed to lick their balls.

In public.

Some people say: 'Yes, but we can do things dogs can't.'

Oh but they can, can dogs.

I assure you they can.

*He takes his coat off and hangs it up.*

**2.**

Listen to this.

I'm standing outside the Housing Association.

About Jackie's mould.

Will I go in, will I not go in?

This limo pulls up.

Big black shiny number.

Darkened windows.

Stops at this young slag's frock shop.

Recognise the limo.

Sir Alec's.

Fuck's he doing here?

He's supposed to be in Edinburgh.

He'll've come back early, I'm thinking.

Out buying a present, he'll be.

A surprise present.

A present for Annabel.

That pure ride of a daughter of his.

Chauffeur out.

Walks round.

Opens the back door.

Where's Sir Alec?

Doesn't get out.

You should see what does.

Tits like chewy toffees.

Bum like marshmallows.

Legs like a pair of airport runways.

It's the daughter.

It's Annabel herself.

I get a fat stonker from here to Inverness and back.

Straight past me, she walks.

Straight past me, into the shop.

Doesn't even see me!

Course she didn't.

I had these on at the time.

*Puts shades on, poses.*

Course I did.

*Takes them off.*

Do youse think I'm a complete bam?


## 3.

Then this wee dog gets out the limo.

It's Wendy.

Annabel's wee dog.

Wee Wendy follows her to the shop door.

But Annabel goes straight in.

Shuts the door in Wendy's wee face.

Then this other dog turns up.

Goes right up to wee Wendy.

Then it speaks.

It says actual words.

To wee Wendy.

It's like: 'Hello, Wendy. How are you getting on?'

And Wendy's like: 'How are you, Cathie?'

So wee Cathie's like: 'I wrote to you, Wendy.

I wrote to you and you didn't write back.'

And Wendy's like: 'Oh, don't take it to heart, Cathie.

I've just been very very busy.'

Then the shop door opens.

Wendy runs in.

Cathie fucks off up the road.

After some old dear.


**4.**

Dogs talking?

Why not?

Dogs saying words?

Dogs have always said words.

Always.

Just like any other wee animal.

That puts its mind to it.


**5.**

Listen to *this*:

Just last week there.

Middle of nowhere.

This loch.

Wee fish in it.

Shot to the surface.

This wee fish.

Shot to the surface and said words.

Actual words.

Out loud.

In a foreign language as well.

No cunt had ever heard of these words.

This wee fish was saying.

Experts brought in.

Translators.

Professors.

Poor wee fish got name-tagged.

Taped.

Filmed.

Computer chip up its arse.

On for months the torture.

Years.

Before these experts came to their final conclusion:

That the words these fish was talking was total and utter gibberish.

So even talking gibberish the animals do it better than we do.

Wouldn't mind learning to speak gibberish myself one day.

Don't suppose it will ever happen.

**Tommy** *puts on his napkin.*

**6.**

So I'm still standing outside the Housing Association.

Will I go in, will I not go in?

This yelping noise.

Look round.

There's wee Cathie.

Running after the old dear.

Catching up with her.

Turning the corner.

I tail them.

Alexander Street.

On to Empire Street.

Up the full length of the Western Boulevard.

Big three-storey mansions.

All the way along it.

Old dear stops at one.

Goes in.

Wee Cathie going in too.

I'm like: 'Heh you, Cathie.

I see wee Wendy's been writing to you.

Did she have any gossip about Annabel?'

Cathie's like: 'Whine growl, whine growl, whine growl, woof.'

And she slinks into the house.

Crafty wee cows.

These dogs.

Chat away to their fellow dogs.

Keep it up for hours.

No problem.

But if it's an actual human being.

If you or I goes up to a dog and talks?

You're blanked.

**Tommy** *picks up his knife and fork.*


**7.**

Didn't bother with the bell.

Because dogs talking's one thing.

But dogs writing?

Could be the next big thing.

Could be.

Because if I could get my hands on a dog's letter.

People would sit up and take notice.

People would see me for what I'm actually are.

They'd see the real me.

The royal me!

**Tommy** *lifts up the cloche. Dog food.*


**Scene Three**

**Tommy**'s *lying on his bed. Watching porn. Sees us, switches TV off and puts down remote.*


**1.**

Do you know why I love the theatre?

Takes you away to Ancient Egypt.

Where royalty knew how to act like royalty.

I mean, say you're depressed and the servants dare to bring you in bad news?

Well, at least you got to batter fuck out of them!


**2.**

Or away to old Russia.

Where nobody ever does fuck all.

Just stay home and shoot theirselves.

In the leg usually.


**3.**

Or away to Ancient Greece.

Where you get to shag your mother.

Or murder your weans.

One or the other.

Away to fuck out of this place.

*He gets up and pulls up his zip.*


**4.**

Take this morning.

Getting ready for my work.

Big fat Jackie's nipping at me.

As usual.

She's like: 'What did the Housing Association say?'

I'm like: 'What did the Housing Association say about what?'

She's like: 'What did the Housing Association say about the mould under the kitchen window?'

I'm like: 'They said they forgot.'

She's like: 'It wasn't the Housing Association that forgot.

Was it, Tommy?'

I'm like: 'Who was it then? Me?'

That shut her up.

Yes, that sent her away.

Away to think again.


**5.**

Into work.

Sir Alec still not back.

Kick fuck out the cleaner.

Get the key.

Nip in to his office.

Sitting there, sitting there.

Think: do something.

There's Sir Alec's laptop!

Staring back at me.

What's it staring at me for?

Open the cunt.

Edinburgh this.

Training for work that.

Department of Social Inclusion the other.

Away to fuck.

Into Sir Alec's drawers.

A binoculars.

Wee bits of shite on the carpet.

Long windy cracks in the ceiling.

All the smudgy fingermarks on the window.

Then.

It's like a beacon.

It's like a beacon shining at you.

Calling you home.

Through all the smudgy fingermarks.

Sir Alec's luxury apartment.

Oh yes.

Straight across the back from the office, you know.

'You see, Tommy,' says Sir Alec.

'What's the point of Mike trailing in from the suburbs every morning?'

(Mike's his chauffeur.)

'Whereas if I get a wee place in town?

That way Mike's only got a two-minute drive.

Feet up the rest of the morning, the guy.'

Know how to treat their staff, eh?

These posh cunts.

**6.**

No sign of Sir Alec though.

Big fuck-off curtains but.

Could be Annabel's room.

That one at the front.

Could be.

Could well be.

If I could get up there.

Get in.

Be all old shampoo bottles.

Old chocolate papers.

Old holey panties.

All the old perfumes of Saudi Arabia.

Big bed there.

Frock lying on the big bed.

Wee frock.

Toty wee frock.

On the great big bed.

Tiny.

Hardly worth wearing.

A duvet.

Duvet under the frock.

Pull back a bit.

Back a bit more.

Another bit more.

More again.

Pull it right back.

Slip in.

Slip right in.

Till you're covered.

She gets in with you.

Just slips in with you.

She's scantily clad.

She's even more scantily clad.

She's like totally scantily clad.

Then it's all snuggly.

Snuggly-wuggly.

Snuggly-snuggly-wuggly.

Yes, Annabel has nothing to fear from me.

I'm the affectionate type.

I like a good cuddle.

Before I shag her senseless.


## 7.

So I'm looking out the window.

Still looking up at Sir Alec's.

Still no sign of him.

Nor Annabel neither.

Hear this voice.

From nowhere.

It's like: 'What are you doing?'

Turn round.

Jesus fucking God, it's Annabel.

Annabel herself!

Looking at me!

Actually looking at me!

Round arse hiding behind her back from me!

Big tits pointing over at me!

Wee panties looking up at me!

And she says it again.

She's like: 'What are you doing?'

I'm like: 'Sir Alec likes me to keep a lookout for him.'

She's like: 'Where is he?'

I'm like: 'Is he not still in Edinburgh, miss?'

She's like: 'Of course he is.

How stupid of me.

I forgot.'

Then she's away.

So I'm like: 'There's no need to leave on my account.

Stay by all means.'

She's like: 'Why would I want to stay with you?'

Like she's offering herself.

Then before I get the chance to say 'Yes please', she's out.

Gone.

Was she coming on to me?

Well, the whole entire office is minging of fanny.

I've got a raving stonker on my hands.

So I think we know the answer.

*Puts on his shades.*

After her!

Down the stairs.

Out.

There she is.

Half way down Stewart Street.

Coming out a newsagent.

She takes off.

Going the other way.

I take off after her.

Top of Stewart Street.

Along High Street.

Round Albert Square.

Right round it.

Round it again.

And again.

Back down High Street.

I've just about caught up with her.

Into the station.

She like vanishes into the station.

Follow her in.

I get in and:

Gone.

*Takes shades off.*

She's gone.

. . . Great, eh?

She must really like me.

It's called playing hard to get.

And that's the thing about class totty like Annabel.

They've got powers, you know.

They've got the power to disappear.

Whereas the Nicolas and the Jackies.

Scum like that.

I wish they would fuckin' disappear.


**8.**

Starving after the hike.

Home for lunch.

Just in the door.

Already Jackie's giving it: 'That's the mould in the bathroom now.'

I'm like: 'You're exaggerating.'

She's like: 'Open your eyes, Tommy.

We're living in a slum.'

I'm like: 'This building won an award.

You're privileged to live in it.'

She's like: 'What was the award for?

Syringes on the stairs?

Burst condoms on the landing?

Or Great Dane shite in the lift?'

I'm like: 'Stick in with me, doll, you'll end up in a castle.'

She's like: 'I'd be quite happy in a house with no mould.'

Don't know what Jackie's problem is with the mould.

The mould is not a problem to me.

Wee moulds.

Growing out the cracks in the walls.

Hanging off the ceiling.

Clinging on round the pipes.

What harm could the wee moulds do?

Friends of mine the wee moulds.

I study them.

Shake their hands.

Kiss them.

And they kiss me back!

Well, it breaks the monotony.


**9.**

Fucked off after that.

Back in to work.

Just got sat down.

Hairy-ears Nicola's in already.

She's like: 'What the fuck are you playing at?'

I'm like: 'Nothing. How?'

She's like: 'You're a middle-aged man.'

I'm like: 'That's a matter of opinion.'

She's like: 'Is it not time you acted your age?'

I'm like: 'What do you mean?'

She's like: 'You've been spotted.

You've been spotted tailing Sir Alec's daughter.'

I'm like: 'How do they know it was me?'

She's like: 'You don't exactly fade into the background in those shades.'

I'm like: 'Who saw me?'

She's like: 'Never you mind who saw you.

What makes you think she'd be interested in you?'

I'm like: 'She came on to me.'

She's like: 'I don't think so somehow.

You're thick as shit.

You're an ugly bastard.

And you're common as muck.'

Don't know who Nicola thinks she's calling ugly.

She's got a face like a whale's plooky arse.

She'll no be laughing when I'm on top.

When it's me telling her what to do.

'Comb my hair with the gaps in your teeth, bitch.'

Who does she think she is?

I've got PhDs in my blood.

My ancestors were dentists.

We were hairdressers to the aristocracy.

We were the aristocracy.

We hobnobbed with royalty.

We were royalty.

And we still are.

Then Nicola's like: 'Sir Alec's been on the phone from Edinburgh. He says you've to take tomorrow off.'

I'm like: 'Did he say why?'

She's like: 'No.'

I'm like: 'I know what it is.

Sir Alec'll be recognising my superiority.'

She's like: 'Your superiority to who?'

I'm like: 'Well, has he given you the day off?'

Now any normal person would lie down and accept defeat.

Am I right?

But not Nicola.

She's like: 'Aye you won't be boasting about your superiority, Tommy, when they put you away.'

I'm like: 'Away where?'

She's like: 'Away where do you think?

Away in the head.'

I'm like: 'You're a halfwit as well as scum, Nicola.

You can't start sending me to my own head.'

She's like: 'You're so right, Tommy.

You're so right.

Because in the place where your head should be, there's nothing there.'

(*Mimicking.*) 'You're so right, Tommy.

You're so right.'

I'll say this for Nicola:

At least she knows when she's beaten.

**Tommy** *gets on bed. Picks up the remote. Goes to switch TV on, but thinks better of it.*

**10.**

That's why I love the theatre.

It gets you away from all the Nicolas and the Jackies.

I actually went tonight.

To this wee theatre.

So I'm sitting there, sitting there.

Watching this wee play.

Tell you what, though.

It's not about Egypt or Russia or Greece.

It's about here.

It's about now.

Who wants to see that shit?

And it's about this wee guy.

Gets off with his boss's daughter at work.

And he's such a prick.

Can't even see there's no future in it.

His boss is going to sack him if he doesn't give her up.

Wee guy goes: 'OK, sack me.'

The boss sacks him.

Cuts off the daughter's money.

She gets sick of the poverty.

Goes back to Daddy.

Wee guy totally loses it.

Breakdown.

Nuthouse.

Wouldny be me.

While she's living back in the lap of luxury?

Oh no.

OK, have a few teary wanks to get over her.

Be all right in hours.

Be roamin' in the gloamin' in hours.

Move on.

Stuff like that:

Just isny real.

Put people off going to the theatre.

And as for those bams from the papers?

Fuckin' loved it.

Och, what do they know?

At the time of their birth God got all their holes mixed up.

One of the wee actresses was a ride, all the same.

I got a roaring stonker.

A big fat one.

A juicy one.

Shut up, shut up.

I'm talking like scum.

Instead of the royalty I'm are.

**Tommy** *switches on TV. Porno resumes playing.*


**Scene Four**

**Tommy** *comes in carrying bags. He sees us and speaks.*


**1.**

Big fat Jackie's nipping at me all morning.

She's like: 'You not going to your work?'

I'm like: 'Sir Alec gave me the day off.'

She's like: 'What for?'

I'm like: 'Must like me.'

She's like: 'What does he like you for?'

I'm like: 'He likes me because he likes me.

Sir Alec's a good guy.

You've got to understand, Jackie: good comes out of good guys like shite and snotters come out of you.'

Then she's like: 'I'm depressed.

I'm fed up.'

I'm like: 'Not again.

I'm going to my work.'

She's like: 'You've got the day off.

What are you going to your work for?'

I'm like: 'To get the fuck away from you.'

I could've said more.

But I didn't like to hurt her feelings.

*He sees he still has the bags and dumps them.*


**2.**

Then I'm at the work.

I'm going in the lift.

Just as hairy-ears Nicola's coming out.

Caked in make-up.

Stinking of perfume.

Then she's like: 'Sir Alec gave you the day off.'

I'm like: 'I want to see him about something.'

She's like: 'He's still in Edinburgh.'

I'm like: 'Still?

How?

Streets of Edinburgh's already paved with gold.

Is he like giving them an extra polish?'

And she's standing like she's barring my way.

So I'm like: 'Out my road.'

She's like: 'There's no point in you going up.

He's given the whole office the afternoon off.'

I'm like: 'I've got work to do.'

She's like: 'What work?'

I'm like: 'I've got work filling out forms.'

She's like: 'What forms is this?'

I'm like: 'What forms do you think?

Forms saying what work I'm doing.'

She's like: 'But you don't do any work.'

I'm like: 'Does all the hair in your ears make you deif, Nicola?

I just said my work *is* filling out forms saying what work I'm doing.'

She's like: 'Aye but what work are you putting in the forms?'

I'm like: 'I just told you.

I'm putting in the forms that I'm filling out the forms.'

Off she fucks.

Beaten again.

I mean what's she like, that Nicola?

She knows work to me is as petrol to tank, tea to gob and spunk to red hot fanny.

**3.**

Get up there.

Entire floor deserted.

Except a wee gang of them.

Bevvying away.

Over in one corner.

**4.**

Into Sir Alec's office.

Sitting there, sitting there.

Thought: Fuck it.

His laptop.

Edinburgh.

Bla bla bla.

Department of Social Inclusion.

Get to fuck.

What's this?

A party?

A party comes up!

On the screen!

At Sir Alec's.

And it's for his birthday!

And it's today.

Now.

Right now.

And it's at his luxury apartment.

Across the back from the office.

Can't be.


## 5.

Binoculars out.

Decorations on the window.

People sitting on the window.

Holding drinks.

Holding cake.

Holding each other!

But Sir Alec would've wanted me there.

He'd've told Nicola to invite me.

And she'll've not bothered her giant manky arse.


## 6.

Wee gang just leaving as I come out the office.

I'm like: 'What's this about a party?'

They're like: 'Are you invited?'

I'm like: 'Of course I'm invited.'

They're like: 'Are you going in that?'

I'm like: 'Of course not.

I'm going home to get dressed first.

Did you think this is the only clothes I've got?'

They're like: 'Yes, we did actually.

And have a bath while you're at it.

You stink.'

I'm like: 'I do not . . .

What of?'

They're like: 'Shite.'

And they all start laughing.

Well, I'm sorry.

But that's just not funny.

My hygiene is second to none.

Wee toothbrush sitting there.

Do my teeth with it, every night.

Then I generally slip it round the back and do my arse as well.


**7.**

Out of there.

Heading home.

These two big dogs walk past.

One's like: 'Would you like to hump me, Fido?'

The other one's like: 'I wouldn't mind, Fifi.'

And head off down a back alley.

And I'm thinking: 'Wish I could get a dog to say that to me . . .

Or even write me a letter.'

Then I'm like: 'Wee Wendy's letters!

Wee Wendy's letters to wee Cathie. They'll get the party
moving.'

Alexander Street.

On to Empire Street.

Up the full length of the Western Boulevard.

Past all the three-storey mansions.

Old dear's house.

Up the path.

Get tore into the doorbell.

Giving it: 'Fuck you.

You doorbell you.'

Old dear appears.

She's like: 'What is it?'

I'm like: 'Your wee Cathie in?'

Looks at me.

Has the nerve to look at me.

Looks at me like I'm some kind of bam.

Me!

That's one of the nicest quietest normalest people you could
ever hope to have met in your entire puff.

Then the wee dog's out.

Wee Cathie.

Bend over to speak to her.

I'm like: 'How's my wee Cathie?'

Sinks her teeth into my nose.

So she does.

Wee cunt.

Turns and runs back into the house.

Follow her in.

She's over at her basket.

She's like: 'Growl growl woof woof get to fuck.'

Head over.

She's like: 'Snarl bark whine keep away from me.'

I'm like: 'What's she so attached to that basket for?'

She's like: 'Girn you bastard you woof.'

I'm like: 'The letters.

She'll be hiding wee Wendy's letters.

In the basket.'

Get over there.

Wee Cathie's like: 'Whine whine snivel don't hurt me.'

Kick her out.

She fucks off.

Lift up the blanket.

Yes!

They all fall out.

Loads of them.

Hunners.

Out of there.

Pick them up and get out of there.

Out on to the Western Boulevard.

Heading home to get changed.

This taxi appears.

And it stops.

For me.

Somebody up there must know something.

Jump in.

Only the driver's going a bit slow.

So I'm like: 'Can you not go any faster?

Come on. Come on.

I'll be late for the party.'

He's like: 'Do you want me to fly?'

I'm like: 'Could you?

Could you fly over the Nicolas and the Jackies?

And I'll flash my arse at them.

And shite on them.

And shout "Dog's letters, dog's letters, dog's letters," at them.'

He's like: 'Get out.'

I'm like: 'What have I done?'

He's like: 'Just get out the taxi.

You're a bam.'

Probably Jackie's brother.

She had thirty-seven brothers, you know.

Thirty-seven at the last count.

She had thirty-seven brothers and every one of them was a taxi driver.


**8.**

Ended up walking the Western Boulevard.

Head held high.

Reading those letters.

Actually reading them.

And:

Biggest disappointment in my life.

Bore, those letters.

Trash.

Turns out dogs are just like people.

Shallow as fuck.

Only capable of writing stuff of interest to other dogs.

Collars hurting them.

The biscuit tin's rusty.

Lamp posts aren't what they used to be.

The odd one or two though.

The odd gem.

'Dear Cathie.

Sorry.

But I can't get used with that totally shite name of yours.

Cathie?

It's so scummy.

Almost as bad as Jackie or Nicola.

Do your owners treat you well?

Annabel is so lovely to me.

She gives me little kisses.

And big kisses.

All over my back.

And all over my front.

Even my front bottom sometimes.

Don't tell anyone. Love Wendy.'

She can kiss my front bottom any time!

And my back bottom!

Or any of my bottoms.

I have a wide selection of kissable bottoms.

For Annabel to choose from!


**9.**

'Dear Cathie.

Annabel's such good fun.

She likes to go out clubbing.

It's true.

And then she comes back at six in the morning.

Mascara all over the place.

Designer dress in shreds.

Stinking of pish and sweat.

Spunk running down her legs.

She's such a slut.

I love her.

Love, Wendy.'

Cheeky cow, that Wendy.

Imagine writing that about Annabel.

Her beloved owner.

I mean: she's top notch, is Annabel.

Access to Sir Alec's limo.

Access to Sir Alec's chauffeur.

Mike.

He fondles her.

Mike does.

All the way up.

All the way.

And she lets him.

No she doesn't.

She's saving herself for me.

To let me fondle her.

No she's not.

She's not like that.

Well, she is a bit.

She is.

She's not.

She is.

Aw what do these dogs know?

I don't even know if I'm reading what I'm reading.

The handwriting of these dogs is diabolical.

'Dear Cathie.

Annabel's in love with Tommy.

And she's too shy to say.

She just follows him around all day.

Sir Alec's busy in Edinburgh.

He's busy arranging a big rise for Tommy.

Tommy's moving to a big mansion on the Western Boulevard.

But even so, Sir Alec still takes time out of his busy schedule!

He phones up Annabel and tells her straight: "If you're in love with Tommy, you must tell him."

You must stop following him around.

You'll get arrested for stalking.'

Love, Wendy.'

Lovely man, that Sir Alec.

There's a couple more good letters.

*He opens the bags and puts on a jacket and hat. Unsuitable fashionwear. Too young for him. Ill-fitting.*

But I've got a party to go to.

Youse scum will have to wait.

*He goes.*


## Scene Five

*The place is in disarray.* **Tommy** *back to normal clothes. Using an umbrella to knight an imaginary figure.*


**1.**

Arise, Sir Murdo.

Arise, Sir Turdo.

No, don't bother arising, Sir Stutter.

Think you're something, don't you?

Just because you own an umbrella.

*He stabs the air with umbrella.*

Well, take that.

And that.

And that.

*He turns and sees us. Puts umbrella down. Comes over to talk.*

It's not as though there was anyone at the party.

All the trash from the work just.

So I'm standing outside Sir Alec's.

Chapping the door, chapping the door.

No answer.

You can hear them all.

Getting tore into pretending to enjoy theirselves.

Chapping the door, chapping the door.

Still nothing.


## 2.

Guy comes up the stairs.

Nods at me.

Who the fuck does he think I am?

Nodding at me.

Carrying an umbrella, he is.

Puts it down.

Rings the bell.

Doesn't seem the umbrella type.

Big lump.

Chest like a tank.

Legs like oil drums.

Nob like a lamp post.

Down to his knees, his nob.

Both knees.

Two nobs.

Guy's got two nobs, for some reason.

Be coming at some poor wee lassie, from both sides.

Looks familiar though.

I'm like: 'Have I seen you before?'

He's like: 'Probably.'

I'm like: 'Who are you?'

He's like: 'Murdo McClean, MSP.

Who are you?'

I'm like: 'Tommy McMillan.

Colleague of Sir Alec's.'

He's like: 'Pleased to meet you.'

And he chaps the door again.

Still no answer.

He's like: 'Waiting long?'

I'm like: 'Not bad.

Hour or so.'

So he's shaking his head.

And goes to knock again.

But the door opens.

Annabel.

She's like: 'Murdo darling.

I thought you weren't coming.

Kiss me.'

Tongue straight down the gob.

Doesn't even ask if I mind.

Ignorant cunt.

Next thing it's hand in hand.

And she's shutting the door after her.

I'm like: 'Excuse me.'

She's like: 'Yes?'

I'm like: 'Am I not getting in?'

She's like: 'Wait a minute.'

And she tells big Murdo to go and get her a champagne.

He fucks off.

Then she's like: 'Well, have you got an invitation?'

I'm like: 'Why would I want an invitation?'

She's like: 'Why wouldn't you?'

I'm like: 'I'm Sir Alec's colleague.'

She's like: 'So is everyone else here.'

I'm like: 'You met me in Sir Alec's office.

Don't you remember me?'

She's like: 'How could I forget you?'

I'm like: 'Exactly. So can I come in?'

She's like: 'Not without an invitation.'

I'm like: 'Could you get Sir Alec?'

She's like: 'What for?'

I'm like: 'It's his birthday.'

She's like: 'I do know that.'

I'm like: 'But he would have wanted me there.'

She's like: 'Not if you haven't got an invitation.'

I'm like: 'But we send each another Christmas cards.'

She's like: 'He sends everyone Christmas cards.'

I'm like: 'But I've got to tell him something.'

She's like: 'Tell me. I'll pass on your message.'

I'm like: 'Well, tell him he's got to stay out of that Edinburgh.'

She's like: 'How?

What's the matter with Edinburgh?'

I'm like: 'The fat bankers will take all his money off him.

And lend it to all the schemie scum.

And the schemie scum won't pay him back.

Then he'll go bankrupt.

And you'll have to go without your slidy panties.'

She's like: 'He'll be in work tomorrow.

Talk to him then.'

I'm like: 'Gonny please let me in.'

She's like: 'I'm very sorry.'

I'm like: 'Och, why not?'

She's like: 'Because you're a disgusting sleazy creep.

I don't care if you're the long-term unemployed.

I don't care how much of a feather in my dad's cap you are.

You've been stalking me for weeks and I'm not putting up with it.'

I'm like: 'I think you're getting me mixed up with someone else.'

She's like: 'Go away.'

I'm like: 'But you've got to let me in.

I've got the very thing you need to liven up this dead loss of a party.'

She's like: 'What's that?'

I'm like: 'Your wee dog Wendy's letters to her wee pal Cathie.'

She's like: 'Everyone says you need treatment.

And if you don't leave me alone, I'll make sure you get it.'

And she shuts the door in my face.

*Beat.*

Annabel, Annabel, Annabel.

You have tits to Timbuktutu.

But you're a jumped-up middle-class twat.

And it would never have worked out between us.

You're a sex-mad trollop.

Whereas I'm the romantic type.


**3.**

So I'm standing there, standing there.

I'm like: 'What am I going to do now?'

Murdo boy's umbrella sitting there.

I'm like: 'Fuck it.

I'm taking it.'

Because you have to feel sorry for Annabel.

Stuck going out with an MSP.

These guys are diabolical.

Middle of a state visit to Seventh Avenue.

Tagging along behind up all these guys in kilts.

Playing the bagpipes.

Representing the nation.

Supposed to be.

And there's all these bankers in suits standing waving flags of Scotland.

Waiting for the king obviously.

Only the king doesny show up.

Cos the king can't afford the cheap flights.

And nobody knows who the fuck the king is.

So all these bankers in suits are standing.

Just standing there.

With their cocks out.

And you know what the MSPs are like.

Right down on their hands and knees.

Sooking away on these cocks.

Cameras flashing.

Then the next day it's all over the TV.

Beamed all over the world.

Turned out the pipers were a shower of drunken bams.

The guys in suits scum from the papers.

Disguised as bankers.

Poor wee Scotland gets humiliated in the eyes of the world again.

All because our MSPs can't tell bankers from scum.

**4.**

Should've known though.

It was all in one of Wendy's letters.

'Dear Cathie.

Annabel's going out with an MSP.

Horrible fat ugly man.

Not a single hair on his whole entire body.

Disgusting.

And she'll regret it.

When I think she could have had that lovely Tommy.

That's training for work.

Actual work.

She's so shallow, Annabel.

She hasn't sussed there's more to Tommy than meets the eye.

And one of these days he's going to come out with it.

Oh yes – all will be revealed.'

Shrewd wee cunts.

These dogs.

Miss nothing.

*He picks up the umbrella. Knighting again.*

Arise Sir Murdo.

Arise Sir Murder.

No, don't bother arising.

I hereby cut off your hands.

I hereby cut off your head.

I hereby cut off your balls.

And eat them.

But they taste shite.

So I spit them out.

And they run away.

Because they're cowards.

Your balls.

Just like you.

So die, ya bastard.

Die.

Die in the name of Scotland.


## Scene Six

**Tommy** *found reading the papers and drinking tea at the table. He turns to us.*


### 1.

That's them decided.

Scotland's to be like the theatre.

All kings and queens.

Hundreds of them.

Running around in tiaras.

Sticking daggers into each another.


### 2.

Oh, they're out looking for the king now.

But they'll be looking for a posh cunt.

They should be looking in the housing schemes.

Up the high flats.

He'll be waiting there for them.

Waiting for the call.

**3.**

Into work earlier.

Right away hairy-ears Nicola's like: 'That's your final warning.

You're suspended.

You can go now.'

I'm like: 'What's my warning for?'

She's like: 'You're three hours late.'

I'm like: 'I am not late.

I'm early.'

She's like: 'How do you work that out?'

I'm like: 'Royalty is never out the house till after lunch.'

I'm like: 'And I'm not going till I see Sir Alec.'

She's like: 'No point in you seeing him. Sir Alec's only been putting up with you because you're living proof the long-term unemployed can get off and stay off the dole.

You were a feather in his cap.

Sorry, Tommy: but you're well out the picture.'

**4.**

Oh Nicola, Nicola.

The hair from your ears hangs down to your titties.

And on down to your padlocked panties.

And up to your armpits where it says 'Hi.'

To all its sweaty wee pals.

Then up and up again.

Back into those hairy ears of yours.

To get mangled in the windmills of your mind.

Never to be seen again.


**5.**

But then appeareth Nicola's bodyguard.

Grabs me.

By the robes.

Escorts me with somewhat violence.

I'm like: 'I'll have you chucked in the dungeons.

And chucked in the sea.

And chucked to the lions.

Who will eat you.

And shit you.

And eat you again.

For ever and ever.

Till you say you're sorry.'

Then Sir Alec walks in.

Sir Alec: to the rescue.

He's like: 'What's going on?

Big Danny's on his way up.

Release that man.'

Which he does.

This big ginger halfwit walks in.

With glasses.

Three pairs.

Must have wanted a right good look at me.

Then all this other lot of trash are in.

Holding cameras.

Sir Alec's like: 'I want to introduce you to Tommy McMillan, Minister.

He's been unemployed for twenty-eight years until he started training for work in the Department.

Tommy, meet the Minister.'

I stick my hand out to shake it, but big Danny walks off.

Sir Alec an' all.

They stand up at the front.

Lights on them.

What the fuck are lights on them for?

Lights should be on me.

Then big Danny's like: 'As you know, we are here to announce the new top man of Scotland.'

And I'm thinking: 'That's me.

My time's come at last.

I'll sleep in a castle tonight.

With Annabel.'

Then Sir Alec's like: 'It gives me great pleasure to announce the new top man is – '

And I jump up to the front.

Just in case some other cunt gets in first.

So I look at Sir Alec and I look at big Danny.

I look at Sir Alec and I look at big Danny.

And I'm like: 'I accept.

I accept.

Cos I'm the king, me.

King Tommy the Second.

Of Scotland.

I'm up to my neck in lineage.

Whereas youse are a bunch of democratically elected nobodies.'

Silence.

Total silence.

The silence to end all silences.

So I'm like: 'Here are my policies.

Firstly, gibberish is to be the language of the entire world.

And firstly I'll take over the banks and run them myself.

I'll be the King of Scotland and the Bank of Scotland.

And firstly training for work in a call centre at the Department of Social Inclusion is to be compulsory for all of youse.

And while I'm shagging every lassie in Scotland youse can all fill out forms saying you're filling out forms.'

So I gave them a couple of wee bows.

And then another couple.

Then just a couple more.

And got the fuck out of there.

Like the royalty I'm are.

**6.**

Midnight when I get home.

Big fat Jackie's in.

She's like: 'You wanting tea?'

I'm like: 'If you're making it.'

She's like: 'What's that on your head?'

I was wearing this at the time.

*Takes out paper crown and puts it on his head.*

I'm like: 'Well, Jackie.

I was at the theatre tonight, you see.

And there's this big actor going round the stage wearing it.

I got up there.

Grabbed it off the usurping cunt.

But he's soldiering on.

Wanting full marks for being a trouper.

He's like: "Tomorrow and tomorrow and tomorrow."

So I'm like: "Aye, aye, aye.

I'll give you it back tomorrow."

Will I fuck.

Evil murdering bastard.

That Macbeth.

Got all the modern kings of Scotland a bad name.'

So Jackie's like: 'There's no such thing as modern kings of Scotland.'

I'm like: 'There is so.

Just because they gave Scotland away for a quick shag in the toilets doesn't mean the line of succession's been cut off.'

She's like: 'Where is he, then?

Who is he?'

I'm like: 'It's me, Jackie.

Me.

I'm the King of Scotland.'

She's like: 'If you're the King of Scotland I'm getting you sectioned.'

I'm like: 'Numptie teatray Isabella,

Shoot your load, your bum's all yella.'

My first-ever words of gibberish.

Didn't even have to try.

Came naturally.

That shut big fat Jackie's big fat gob.

But she was evil to the end.

She never even brought me in my tea!


## 7.

Next day this guy turns up at the door.

With two heids.

He's got two heids.

No, three.

Or was it four?

Well, they were all very nice heids.

But something weird about him, all the same.

Only I can't work out what it was.

In he comes.

Sits down.

Says nothing.

Just looks at me.

With all those nice heids of his.

Takes out pen and paper.

So I'm like: 'Of course.

He's come to interview me.

For King of Scotland.'

Only no actual questions were asked.

Just listens.

Takes notes.

So I'm like:

'I should be King of Scotland because I can do royal waving.

And I can make foreigners unwelcome with the best of them.

And I can tell old-age pensioners to fuck off.'

Still no questions.

Just kept on with the notes.

So I'm like:

'Tillietudlem help ma boab.

Bollocking scrivens suck my nob.'

More notes.

More.

So I'm like – (*Aggressively.*) 'Have I got the job or not?'

So he's like: 'You'll be hearing from us within days.'

And fucks off.

Cagey cunt.

Well, you've got to be careful who you give King of Scotland to.

They're all after that job.

Which is too bad.

Because it's my name that's on it.

*He goes back to his paper and his tea, still with his crown on.*

## Scene Seven

*A secure room in a mental hospital.* **Tommy** *in a straitjacket. Hums 'Up Up and Away'.*

### 1.

Actually a horse and carriage they sent.

They shut down the M8 motorway for the day.

Be a major sacrifice for a modern industrialised nation.

Luckily Scotland isn't one.

Not that Scotland's a banana republic either.

Oh no.

Because Scotland's a banana.

### 2.

Crowds waving at me all along the route to Edinburgh.

Seemingly.

I couldn't see them.

Horse and carriage was fortified.

To prevent assassination attempts.

**3.**

Turns out Edinburgh Castle's actually quite a long way from Edinburgh.

Out in the middle of nowhere somewhere.

Lovely people though.

Uninhibited.

And some very accomplished speakers of gibberish.

A joy to listen to.

*As if struggling to pronounce it:*

Shoogly bau –

Shooglybauchly –

Shooglybauchlyrumpty tumptyknickety knocketyknoo

Granny Grey's got a baldy heid

And she did a giant –

She did a giant –

She did a –

Haven't quite cracked it yet.


**4.**

Terrible burden being King of Scotland.

Well, I'm popular with the tourists.

But the cheek you've to take off them.

They're like: 'No, I don't want your autograph.'

I'm like: 'Why not?'

They're like: 'Because you are not the King of Scotland.

You've been locked up cos yer aff yer heid.

Yer in the asylum.'

So I'm like: 'If this is the asylum how come there's no asylum-seekers?'

**5.**

And that big fat Jackie's been trying to get in beside me.

So I wrote her a nice wee letter.

I'm like: 'Jackie.

Great being King of Scotland.

The clothes is all the latest fashion.

Cutting-edge seemingly.

Bit tight round the shoulders.

And if you're very good and don't shout out when it hurts they shove champagne cocktails up your arse.

Then they ask you to do it to them.

They love it.

So sorry, Jackie, but you can't join me.

They're keeping me away from scum like you.

But if you could post me in a cup of tea I'd be grateful, Tommy.'

**6.**

So any minute now they'll be coming for me.

They will.

They'll be coming for me.

*He struggles to his feet.*

They're taking me on a tour of my nation.

And they'll be keeping me away from the scum.

Yes, they'll be taking me up up and away.

In my beautiful balloon.

Away over the sky towers of damp and of mould.

Up over the golden beaches of rubber and of excrement.

Round by the silver estates of Wimpey and of Barratt.

Sweeping past the alleys of methadone and of crack.

Oh you beautiful nation.

Of the lottery terminals.

And the prisons.

And the politicians in the prisons.

The ones that got the jail for fiddling their expenses.

And of the nursing homes.

And the old dears in the nursing homes.

Look at that one there.

The one between the buggered stereo and the plate of cold soup.

That's my mammy.

My Scottish mammy.

I love you, Mammy.

I love you.

So please come in your wheelchair.

Sail in your wheelchair.

Drive.

Take wings.

Fly in your wheelchair.

To be with me tonight.

Because the treatment I'm getting is –

It's an absolute –

It's –


**7.**

So, people of Scotland.

Could youse not rise up.

Stand together.

As one nation.

Shout high and low.

Write to your MSP.

Sign a petition.

Shame the government.

Anything.

But get me a budgie.

Be nice, a wee pet.

Be company.

*He is joined by a choir of budgies.*

**The End**

# The Tobacco Merchant's Lawyer

A play for one actor

*The Tobacco Merchant's Lawyer* premiered at Oran Mor, Glasgow, in 2008, and featured the following cast:

**Enoch Dalmellington**   John Bett

*Director*   Liz Carruthers

**Character**

**Enoch Dalmellington**, *a lawyer in his fifties*

**Setting**

The attic workroom of Mr Dalmellington in late eighteenth-century Glasgow, prior to the American War of Independence.

**One**

*A large desk piled with work and a chair. Map of Scotland, a drawing of Edinburgh Castle and a drawing of Euphemia,* **Dalmellington**'s *daughter.*

**1.**

*Behind the desk* **Dalmellington** *works. Tray of food to one side. After a few seconds he stops and goes to listen at the door. He comes back and sniffs at his food.*

**2.**

Widow MacKay brought up some nourishment on a tray.

Much needed.

I've been at my accounts two days and nights.

**3.**

The price of pews at the Tron Kirk – thirteen guineas per annum.

For myself and my daughter Euphemia.

Says I to Euphemia: 'The price of God is sky-high these days.

We can no longer afford to pray in the kirk.'

'Then we will pray at home,' says she.

And a further five guineas for the new roof levy.

Says I to Euphemia: 'The price of new roofs has gone through the roof.'

I needn't have aspired to drawing laughter.

She's a dreich pious humourless girl – that daughter of mine.

For which blessing I must thank God.

Her dreich pious humourless outlook counteracts my excess of levity.

## 4.

Then there's eleven shillings for coal.

And nineteen shillings for books.

I should have a word with Euphemia about the latter.

Or perhaps I'll eschew that conversation.

For disappointment in the face of your bookish only daughter is a pain not to be contemplated.

## 5.

The meal was prepared by Euphemia.

And comprehensively and heartlessly criticised by Widow MacKay.

The good lady found it wanting in temperature.

And moisture.

And texture.

And appearance.

And odour.

And quantity.

And flavour.

'The bird has been baked dry,' says Widow MacKay.

'And the turnips have been boiled to a paste.'

'Practice makes perfect,' says I.

'Well, I hope it makes perfect in haste, Mr Dalmellington,' says she.

'Or you will have many months of stomach ailments.'

## 6.

*He tucks in. It becomes obvious he's not enjoying it and he stops.*

## 7.

I did question Euphemia on why she is taking over Widow MacKay's duties in the kitchen.

'In our financial predicament,' says she, 'this must be but the first step to taking over *all* the household duties.'

'Would you not be better,' says I, 'accepting the first suitable offer of marriage?'

'I have no wish to leave you, Father,' says she.

'But who will protect you when I am gone?' says I.

'God will protect me,' says she.

'But if my father wishes me to marry it is my duty to obey him.'

It is all very well Euphemia adopting a noble self-sacrificing stance.

But as a widower it is *my* duty to be a father *and* a mother to my daughter.

And speaking, therefore, as a *mother*, I am entirely unable to see my daughter suffer.

## 8.

I did have it in mind just now to advise Widow MacKay of some household economies.

But she distracted me – as is so often the case – by repeating the bizarre sayings of the fortune-teller, the Mistress Zapata of Grahamston.

## 9.

*He goes over to the door for a few seconds before returning.*

## 10.

Widow MacKay is never done reporting Mistress Zapata's prophecies and grandiose visions.

'One day the city of Glasgow will extend as far as the eye can see.

And it will house a million souls.

And the beautiful local stone will be turned black.

As indeed will be the beautiful River Clyde.

And there will be a cathedral of education.

Located on a hill.

Above the Kelvin River away out in the west.'

'But we have a perfectly adequate university quadrangle not eight hundred yards away on the High Street,' says I.

'Oh, but Mistress Zapata says the High Street will go into a serious decline,' says she.

'It will become a hotbed of the prostitution.

Which will be a sore temptation for the student population.

Who will succumb to epidemics of the syphilis.

And not only that,' says she.

'When the university moves to the hill in the west there will be women attending its classes.'

'And how will the good ladies reach this mountainous western location?' says I.

'By way of horseless carriages,' says she.

'Is the good lady suggesting,' says I, 'that these carriages will advance by means of their own locomotion?'

'Won't it be a wonder?' says she.

'It will indeed be a wonder,' says I. 'And proof positive that these prophecies are nothing but charlatanry.

And please say nothing further to Euphemia.

Or you'll have her pining for this Utopia.'

In truth Euphemia is a devotee of reason herself.

She would be extremely dismissive of this charlatan's ravings.

But these visions of women attending classes precisely expresses Euphemia's most fervent wish.

And it would be cruel to have them repeated in her company.


## 11.

A singular drawback of Mistress Zapata – I should point out – is her residency in the village of Grahamston.

Hard by Glasgow as it is, Grahamston and yourselves *may well* not be acquainted.

(And fortunate for you if you aren't.)

It is located at the end of Virginia Street here.

Turn right along Argyle Street.

Past Queen Street, Buchanan Street and Union Street.

But stopping short of Hope Street you'll find what looks little more than an alley.

Turn up there and the way will open out into Alston Street, the principal thoroughfare of Grahamston.

(If it may be dignified with that description.)

Alongside the grandeur of Glasgow's principal thoroughfares:
the Trongate, the Briggait, the High Street and the
Gallowgate – all much admired by visiting scribblers –
Alston Street presents a shabby face to the world.

Indeed, it remains not entirely paved!

Widow MacKay often returns from this Grahamston muddied.

'Muddied but unbowed,' says she.

Says I to Widow MacKay: 'Why, only round the corner on
the Trongate the tobacco merchants parade daily in their
ermine robes and powdered wigs. And you return from the
muddy tracks of Grahamston bespattered and besmirched.
What if you are recognised?'

'Yes, and strip these tobacco merchants of their robes and
wigs,' says she, 'and they will have the same mud splatters as
the rest of us.'

'But the tobacco merchants would never allow themselves to
be seen on Alston Street,' says I.

'Indeed they have a *theatre* on Alston Street – and it's clearly
visible!'

'Oh I've a notion a few of your tobacco merchants have seen
the inside of a few theatres in their time,' says she.

And with that final piece of effrontery off parades the
MacKay phenomenon before I can further contradict her
aberrations.


**12.**

*He goes to the door to listen before returning.*

## 13.

Euphemia has *another* suitor in with her.

Master George Buccleuch intends to propose.

In spite of marriage to my daughter being his dearest wish it did take a quantity of persuasion to hurry him in.

He's convinced my charming daughter is a sort of ogress who will callously reject his offer.

Her reputation as a refuser of men goes before her.

I'm not hopeful for him.

Euphemia joined me last night.

Reminding me we dwell in a backward-looking society.

With its tendency to frown on female attendance at the seats of learning.

I said that perhaps ladies should be allowed in to stand at the seats of learning.

Or I would have said, had it not been more of my levity than my daughter could bear.

So the next best thing, according to Euphemia, was to live here for ever and to look after me, the very best of fathers.

Whereupon, speaking as a mother, I was quite unable to speak.

For I could not bring myself to remind my daughter that her housekeeping leaves a considerable amount to be desired.

## 14.

Master Buccleuch has returned these six weeks from a stay in the American colonies.

He had been sponsored, through family connections, by Mr McCorquindale – the leading tobacco merchant – to learn the tobacco trade.

The boy's return is substantially earlier – by some four and a half years – than had been predicted.

The circumstances of his return – to date – are somewhat mysterious.

## 15.

Then there is the question of his beliefs.

Says he: 'All men are equal.'

'Yes,' says I, 'excepting the black man, of course.'

'Excepting none, Mr Dalmellington,' says he.

'But the latest authors are in agreement that the black man is an inferior species, closer to the apes,' says I.

'At least they were agreed when I last read them.

And that's not even three decades ago.'

'The slaves should be set free,' says he.

'Yes,' says I. 'You may go in to my daughter now.'

Well, his reasoning powers may be deficient but the boy is sincere and spirited.

And much good will it do him with Euphemia.

## 16.

*He goes to the door, listens, and returns.*

## 17.

The alert among you will have noted I did say American *colonies*.

This was from habit.

The United States are now challenging for their independence and may soon be so.

Unlike our own dear Scotland, tethered these seventy years.

Of course independence for Scotland is not a respectable topic of conversation.

Small back-street lawyers such as myself must keep quiet about our opinions.

Until that day when Scotland and the United States may trade freely.

And the Scottish Lion roars again.

## 18.

*He listens at the door again and returns.*

## 19.

What is keeping them?

I may really wait no longer.

## 20.

While I have hoped and prayed – and prayed and hoped – Euphemia will one day say yes to a suitable suitor, her constant refusals have forced me to act.

I was advised, in short, to invest in the importation of tobacco.

Such were the profits being reported that – if true – there is no doubt Euphemia's future would have been secured.

And that I, Enoch Dalmellington, might consider myself a tobacco merchant and parade up and down the Trongate daily, resplendent in my ermine robe and my powdered wig.

Ho ho.

## 21.

Old Mr McCorquindale, the tobacco merchant, had recently returned from America after twenty years, rich beyond our wildest dreams.

He'd heard that I was looking to invest my fifteen hundred guineas.

Accordingly he called round and offered me the chance to invest the entire sum in a tobacco trading venture.

Says I to Mr McCorquindale:

'Thank you for the opportunity to invest my fortune.

But should your ship lose the goodwill of God I will lose my entire investment on a solitary mission.'

'But it is not a solitary mission,' says he.

'It is *three separate missions*.

The voyages of the *Port Glasgow*, the *Dumbarton* and the *Baltimore*.

And such is my confidence I myself am travelling aboard the *Baltimore*.'

'Congratulations, Mr Dalmellington,' says he, when I signed the contract.

'On my return from America I fully expect your daughter and yourself to move into one of the new houses in St Andrew's Square, where you will receive the best families in the city.'

And so it was that the *Port Glasgow*, the *Dumbarton* and the *Baltimore* dropped anchor off the coast of the small island of Santa Katerina before heading north to fill their hulls with Virginian tobacco.

It was here they were attacked by the infamous pirates of the Caribbean.

It's now a full six months since the ships were lost.

Old Mr McCorquindale has still not returned.

Nor have I heard a word from him.

And far from being *separate* missions the *Port Glasgow*, the *Dumbarton* and the *Baltimore* were reported in the *Herald* as having travelled in *convoy*, put down their anchors *together* and were known by the colourful expression 'sitting ducks'.

Only one thing comforts me in this sorry business.

The said pirates of the Caribbean may presently be enjoying a degree of infamy.

But in the centuries to come their exploits will be forgotten as surely as a shipwreck at the bottom of the ocean.


## 22.

I have an appointment with Grimond the accountant in Candleriggs Street for a discussion on the merits of bankruptcy.


## 23.

**Dalmellington** *puts his coat on.*


## 24.

Shameful as it is to lose a modest family fortune I can take comfort only in there being worse offences.

The Provost Buchanan was removed from office for the embezzlement of city funds.

And he had a street named after him!


## 25.

*He goes out.*

## Two

*Dinner plates have been cleared away.*

### 1.

**Dalmellington** *comes in and takes his coat off.*

### 2.

Disaster averted.

God is on the side of the pious majority after all.

### 3.

(*Calls out.*) Euphemia.

Euphemia!

### 4.

He's never *still* in there with her!

I can't see what difference *hours* of importuning will make.

Her answer will still be a resounding negative.

### 5.

Such splendid offices on Candleriggs Street: Grimonds the accountants.

In spite of which splendour I dithered hither and thither.

But whether hither or thither took the upper hand in the dithering I would not like to venture!

## 6.

Thirteen times I turned into Candleriggs Street.

And thirteen times I turned back on to the Trongate.

And on the thirteenth time whom should I encounter?

Old Mr McCorquindale himself, newly back from the West Indies.

And sweeping back and forth, he is – not to mention hither and thither – in animated conversation with all and sundry in his ermine robe and powdered wig standing in the sharpest contrast to my shabby vestments.

'Och Dalmellington, what bad luck!' says McCorquindale.

'A one in a thousand misfortune that this should befall such as yourself – who is without the healthy spread of investments of such as myself.'

'But Mr McCorquindale, sir, you informed me that I *had* made three separate investments,' says I.

'And now I read that the ships were travelling *in convoy*, that they put down their anchors together and they were known by the colourful expression *sitting ducks*.'

'The decision to travel in convoy,' says he, 'was taken by the ship's captain and reflects the very latest thinking in defensive manoeuvres.'

'And what became of their "extensive and unique *defence* capability"?'

'The wrong crew had been taken on by the captains,' says he.

'For they knew not how to man the guns.'

'You mean the guns lay idle while the ships burned?' says I.

'I do,' says he.

'And how came it that you managed to survive the disaster?' says I.

'Why I,' says he, 'had the good fortune to be on the island of Santa Katerina engaged in selling the ship's cargo.'

I was left most dissatisfied with these so-called answers and would have protested further, whereupon he rushed on with:

'And how is your Euphemia?

Still unmarried?'

What a true gentleman Mr McCorquindale is!

To be away all that time and *remember* my daughter's marital status as the principal vexation of my life!

Even *above* my finances!

'Why Master George Buccleuch is in proposing marriage to her as we speak,' says I.

'But any marriage of Euphemia to George Buccleuch would be a disaster,' says he.

'For the boy was a most ungrateful passenger.

Constantly complaining of homesickness or seasickness or can't be bloody bothered sickness.

And as if these offences against the masculine gender were not sufficient, all the while protesting the slaves should be treated like *normal human beings*!'

'Worry not, Mr McCorquindale,' says I, 'my Euphemia has refused much better prospects than Master George Buccleuch.'

## 7.

And then – thank God – on hearing of the direness of my situation this best of men says to me:

'You, sir, will *not* go bankrupt.

I will pay the interest on your debts.

I will take ownership of your house.

And you will continue your residence in your beloved Virginia Street.'

'To continue our residence in Virginia Street after all?' thinks I.

It was all I could do to restrain myself from embracing old Mr McCorquindale.

## 8.

At which point in our perambulation himself and I reached the architectural wonders and noble prospects of Glasgow Cross.

Whereupon we entered the Tontine inn to sample the coffee.

I must confess to surprise at the *extent* of McCorquindale's smoking habit.

'Tobacco has such a delightful fresh healthy aroma,' says he.

'It is reminiscent of the hot southern sun.

Here, try it for yourself,' and he blew the stuff straight into my face.

And exploded into guffaws of merriment.

A joke, I realised at once.

A joke perhaps better suited to his colleagues aboard ship.

But a joke nonetheless.

I would have laughed but I was too busy choking on the fumes.

## 9.

*He goes to the door, listens and returns.*

**10.**

Widow MacKay detains me on my return just now.

Herself just returned from the abode of Mistress Zapata.

'There will one day be small box receptacles.

Which will stand in every drawing room in the land.

And in these receptacles will appear the town crier.

Who will bespeak his proclamations from this same box receptacle.

And not just to the city.

But to the nation!'

Says I to Widow MacKay: 'Every home in the land is to have its own town crier?'

'Why no,' says she, 'it will be *the same* town crier.

Appearing at every home in the land.'

'And what height will this town crier be that a small box receptacle will contain him?' says I.

'He will be but five inches tall,' says she.

'And at the end of the proclamation,' she went on, 'he will not take his leave.

Neither via the front nor the back door.

For he will vanish into thin air.'

Says I to Widow MacKay: 'You speak as though you relish the prospect of these scarifying havers.'

Or so I would have said had she not retreated *in triumph* into her kitchen.


**11.**

Ah – that sounds like Master Buccleuch emerging now.

**12.**

*He goes to go, but turns back.*

**13.**

Ah!

I believed I omitted to inform you that according to the Mistress Zapata the smoking of tobacco will one day be *banned in public places.*

Is it not hard to credit that the charlatan would try to get away with such barefaced effrontery?

It is a truth universally acknowledged that the tobacco plant will be responsible for a substantial improvement in the health of the nation.

*He goes.*

**Three**

**Dalmellington** *at work.*

**1.**

*He looks up at us.*

The rarely used term 'discombobulation' would barely suffice.

My only daughter Euphemia has replied to Master George Buccleuch's proposal *in the affirmative.*

**2.**

'But why, darling daughter?' says I to Euphemia.

'First and foremost,' says she, 'because you are my father.'

'What's that got to do with it?' says I.

'Why because you approve of him, of course,' says she.

'What gave you that idea?' says I.

'Well, you sent him in to me.

Why, do you *not* approve of him?'

'I'm unresolved on the matter,' says I.

'You're unresolved?' says she.

'He and I are insufficiently acquainted,' says I.

'You're *insufficiently acquainted* and yet you sent him in to me?' says she.

'What don't you like about him?'

'He is not always spoken of highly,' says I.

'Pray who did not speak of him highly?' says she.

'Well, he did let elderly Mr McCorquindale down,' says I.

'He was incensed by the treatment of the slaves,' says she.

'Well, the slaves are not guests at the Tontine Inn,' says I.

'They should not be whipped and starved,' says she.

'They are human beings.'

'They are an inferior species,' says I. 'Closer to the apes.'

'Slavery should be abolished forthwith!' says she.

'And who says so?' says I.

'Father – the latest authors are quite clear on the matter,' says she.

'Oh they are?' says I.

'Yes they are,' says she.

'And it was so difficult for poor Master Buccleuch to stand up in front of the whole crew and state his case.

And then they made him *walk the plank*!

So he had to swim the many miles to the shore through *shark-infested waters*.'

'Well, there's no condoning such inhumane conduct,' says I.

'But the latest authors are really now saying the black race are equal?'

'Yes, they are,' says she.

'Well, that will require a modicum of getting used to,' says I.

'And do you still disapprove of Master Buccleuch?' says she.

'Why no,' says I.

'Barely out of boyhood.

Swimming against the tide of opinion to stand up for the ideas of the latest authors.

And then being required to . . . take his chances in the waters.

With the . . . creatures of the sea.

I approve of him very much indeed.'

'Well, he's waiting to talk to you,' says she.


**3.**

I was so dazed with the foregoing I almost omitted to bring Euphemia up to date.

'Virginia Street is saved,' says I, from the door.

'How is this possible?' says she.

'God is merciful,' says I.

'God is indeed merciful,' says she.

'But it is not his usual custom to write cheques.'

'Dearest daughter,' says I, 'are you aware a joke passed from your lips?'

Or I would have said if she had not rushed in with:

'Tell me about God's mercy later.

Master Buccleuch is waiting.'

## 4.

But on my way next door to join Mr Buccleuch I had the
misfortune to run into Widow MacKay agog with the latest
outpouring of the Grahamston medium.

'Grahamston will be swept away as Glasgow advances,'
says she.

'Now those,' says I, 'are the first sensible words Mistress
Zapata has uttered.'

'And in its place,' says she, 'there will be a new carriage
station of cathedral-like proportions.

The Central Carriage Station.

And the carriages will run on iron rails with hot clouds
trailing behind as they go.'

'Not dissimilar,' says I, 'to the hot clouds trailing behind
Mistress Zapata.'

Or I would have said had not Widow MacKay not gone on to
new absurdities.

'And Glasgow – ' she went on, 'the most beautiful small city in
these Islands – will one day be razed to the ground and
replaced by buildings of so many storeys that the summits
may not be seen by the naked eye.

Due to a new fashion of water closets being required in every
household, *even for the poor*.'

I refrained from protesting.

Instead I made a point which I thought more telling.

'Can you tell the Mistress Zapata to confine herself to affairs of the heart?

And listening out for voices from the other side?

Instead of making foolish predictions about the future advancement of the City of Glasgow.'

'Mistress Zapata,' says Widow MacKay, 'does not consider herself parochial.

Rather she is fully apprised of the wider world.

And indeed is often described as an political medium.'

'And what,' says I, 'is there to interest such as *you* in the wider world?'

'Mr Dalmellington,' says she.

'Since the death of Mister Mackay the wider world is my *sole* interest.'

And with that the good lady highstepped ceremoniously into her kitchen.

If this were anyone else I might have shed a tear or two of sympathy.

But the ferocity and venom of the widow left me . . . entirely . . . unmoved!


**5.**

Indeed I was still shaking with mirth at the recollection of *water closets for the poor* when I entered the chamber where Mr Buccleuch awaited me.

'And what is amusing you?' says he.

'Oh passing levities,' says I.

'Passing levities.'

'Are you certain it's not that I am too laughable to marry your daughter?' says he.

'Not at all,' says I.

'You are a very worthy partner for my daughter, standing up for your principles as you do.

But do recall – for future reference – that not everyone will have read the latest authors on the subject of slavery.

Unlike such as ourselves perhaps.'

'It doesn't take reading to recognise human suffering,' says he.

'But not all of us are equipped to recognise suffering when we see it,' says I.

'Oh, but some suffering is entirely obvious,' says he.

'Exactly what form of suffering did you see?' says I.

'Is Mr McCorquindale your friend?' says he.

I chose my words carefully for his young ears.

Says I: 'Mr McCorquindale is my business colleague.

Do you have a complaint against him?'

'I don't want to discuss Mr McCorquindale,' says he.

Feeling that Master Buccleuch was holding something back, says I to him: 'Have you anything else to say for yourself?' says I.

At this the young gentleman hemmed and hawed.

And hawed and hemmed.

And turned red in the face.

And looked at the ceiling.

And looked at the floor.

And out of the window.

Till finally I persuaded him to mumble out a few words.

'I cannot marry Euphemia until I find a hundred guineas,' says he.

'A hundred guineas?' says I.

'Where would you be hoping to get it?'

'From you,' says he.

'From me?' says I.

'Well, you're rich lawyer, sir,' says he.

'And you have a house on Virginia Street – on four floors.

And I will soon be a part of the family,' says he.

'I am far from being rich,' says I.

But it was clear he did not believe me.

'I don't believe you,' says he.

'And I just don't understand why you want me to be your son-in-law, yet you have ambitions to destroy my life.

So the marriage is hereby cancelled.'

I was about to tell him to lower his voice or my daughter would overhear.

But Mr Buccleuch had run out.

I was about to follow whereupon my daughter rushed in.

'You must seize this chance of happiness from such a suitable young gentleman,' says I.

'But I heard him cancel the marriage,' says she.

'This was but in the heat of the moment,' says I.

'And do not worry – I'll borrow the hundred guineas.'

'Who from?' says she.

I refrained from answering.

For in truth I knew not.

## 6.

At which juncture old McCorquindale arrived.

With him was all the paperwork for me to sign the house over.

A clause had been included to restrict Euphemia and myself to the attic and upper two floors of Virginia Street.

'The previous arrangement,' says he, 'was unfavourable to my interest.'

'In what way?' says I.

'To defray some of the cost of the enterprise I would require to sub-let the lower floors,' says he.

'Mr McCorquindale,' says I, 'my daughter and I have lived our entire lives on all four floors of Virginia Street.'

'Without such a clause,' says he, 'I must regrettably terminate the agreement and leave you to face bankruptcy alone.'

And so it was with heavy heart I picked up the pen.

Seeing my hand tremble as I signed, Mr McCorquindale kindly invited me to join him in a celebration.

But with the loss of the lower floors of Virginia Street I thought it unlikely that I would have the required appetite.

However it would provide an early opportunity to request a loan for Master Buccleuch.

And so it came about that I strolled with dolorous heart alongside Mr McCorquindale along the Trongate into Argyle Street.

Past Queen Street.

And Buchanan Street.

And Union Street.

Where could the old tobacco merchant be taking me?

At which point we turn into . . . Alston Street.

And Grahamston.

It was here that old Mr McCorquindale met some former colleagues.

Dating back to his time as a humble apprentice of carpentry.

And company more lacking in education, fashionable attire and personal hygiene it would be hard to imagine.

Nevertheless the drinks flowed all night and all night Mr McCorquindale made us laugh till we could laugh no more.

His many jests at my expense were hilarious.

Indeed after five stoups of ale and five gills of whisky the loss of the lower floors of Virginia Street and the loan for Mr Buccleuch receded into insignificance.

The revelry reached its peak when it was required of me that I perform a monkey dance.

Which I performed with gay abandon.

Much to the merriment of the entire establishment.

'To make such an idiot of yourself, Mr Dalmellington!

You have given us our best laugh in many a long year,' was a typical comment of Mr McCorquindale's colleagues, who, for all their rough manners, were indeed prime examples of the expression 'salt of the earth'.


## 7.

The sole darker note was our return to Virginia Street.

McCorquindale – much the worse for wear – was wont to challenge every passing hooligan to a brawl.

It was our good fortune that we returned to Glasgow under cover of darkness.

Mr McCorquindale's bleeding face, askew wig and tattered ermine robe would not have been noticed by many.

**8.**

*He goes over to door and returns.*

**9.**

Nothing has been heard of Mr Buccleuch since yesterday.

I am expecting him to put in an appearance.

But it's early still.

**10.**

*He hears something.*

Or is that him now?

*He listens.*

Yes, I believe that is his voice.

Coming in from the street.

**11.**

But if I may detain you for one second longer with Mistress Zapata's latest preposterous outpouring.

Apparently Virginia Street will one day be a cauldron of rampant sodomy.

Men will be seen in the street holding hands.

Kissing.

And further unseemly activity.

'My beloved Virginia Street given over to sodomy?' says I.

Or I would have said had not Widow MacKay's face jetted forth in tears.

'Why, what is wrong?' says I.

'It was Mister MacKay,' says she.

'He was mistaken for a sodomite.

And brutally murdered.'

'Why Widow MacKay,' says I, 'I had no idea.'

And I leaned forward to comfort the good lady.

Whereupon she looked me in the eye all too briefly.

. . . All too briefly?

Did I say 'all too briefly'?

What can be the meaning of 'all too briefly'?

But whether briefly or no the good lady looked me in the eye *again* and rushed from the scene.


## 12.

*He goes to go and comes back.*


## 13.

I did make a mental note to say nothing to Euphemia on the subject of Mister MacKay's death.

And sodomy.

But knowing my daughter as I do I feared she might rebuke me.

And point out that the latest authors were advising that sodomy was now a bona-fide activity and *encourage* its practice.

**Four**

**Dalmellington** *at work. He is clearly not concentrating and several attempts to work fail. He stops 'finally' and turns to look at us.*

### 1.

Widow MacKay has just been up.

'Old Mr McCorquindale,' says she, 'did pass me on Trongate.

You are to call round in an hour's time.'

'Thank you,' says I, and observed that Widow MacKay did not take her leave with her customary bruising abruptness.

'Did I not observe you in the village of Grahamston the other night?' says she.

'It has gone from my mind,' says I.

'Which night was this?'

'I was taking my leave of Mistress Zapata,' says she.

'You were making your way into the Corn Exchange Tavern.'

'Quite correct, Widow MacKay,' says I.

'I allowed myself to be taken on a mystery excursion.'

'I'd believed you were not enamoured of Grahamston,' says she.

'I have been wrong about Grahamston all along,' says I.

It is a most convivial place and I will be sorry to see it displanted by the Central Carriage Station.'

'I will be sorry too,' says Widow MacKay.

And as she made to go out it came to me that these were the tenderest words to have passed between myself and Widow MacKay in the twenty years since Mister MacKay passed away.

'Widow MacKay,' says I, 'I am most curious to know which affairs of the wider world in particular draw you to the sayings of Mistress Zapata.'

'The affairs,' says she, 'of my country.'

And with that remark instead of walking out she hiked up her petticoats.

Revealing in the process a thigh of impressive shapeliness.

And just as I thought the good lady's petticoats could rise no further appeared . . . a garter.

In the tartan.

In the tartan of the clan of her husband.

Whereupon the good lady replaced her petticoat, before *sauntering* out with a *swagger* in her *gait*!


## 2.

And as she went I recalled a saying of the Mistress Zapata.

It was to the effect that the legs of women would one day be on permanent public display.

And it would be considered the right of the female sex.

I was outraged.

Now, however, I wonder if there is something in such displays.

And I made a note to consult the latest authors on whether women's legs *should* be on permanent display.

In the interest of the rights of the female sex.


## 3.

Mr Buccleuch put in an appearance this morning.

'My humblest apologies for yesterday,' says he.

'Granted,' says I.

'Euphemia will never forgive me,' says he.

'Nonsense,' says I.

'You are a future member of the family.'

'So will you repay the debt then?' says he.

'I am unable to,' says I.

'I wouldn't mind,' says he.

'But I'm being vastly overcharged.'

'I could act as your legal representative,' says I, 'and attempt to have the charges reduced.

A strongly worded letter perhaps?

If I may but know to whom you owe the money.'

At which point he once again hemmed and hawed.

And stared at the floor.

'Mr Buccleuch,' says I, 'I insist you inform me.

Otherwise I will not be able to assist you.'

'I owe the money,' says he, 'to Mr McCorquindale.'

'In that case,' says I, 'I'm sure the costs are perfectly justified.'

'One hundred guineas for my upkeep during the voyage?' says he.

'And my training aboard ship?

And the cost of my return passage?

Why, that shouldn't be more than twenty guineas.'

Whereupon I heard Mr McCorquindale's arrival.

I did not deem it politic to continue the arithmetical debate with Master Buccleuch.

So I ushered the boy out by the back stairs.

**4.**

And rushed straight down to find that the tobacco merchant was already in, speaking with Euphemia.

And the door was closed.

As I swithered whether to join the assembly my only daughter emerged.

'Please don't ever require me to see that hooligan again,' says she.

'He is *drunk*!'

'Ah!' says I.

'And he asked me to be his live-in housekeeper,' says she.

'Well, he does not yet know of your betrothal to Master Buccleuch,' says I.

'To be the live-in housekeeper of an unmarried man,' says she, 'amounts to being his whore!'

'Knowing Mr McCorquindale as I do,' says I, 'I am certain you must have misunderstood his meaning.'

Or I would have said had Euphemia not rushed out with 'Get the hooligan away from me.

Get the hooligan away from me!'

It was my unavoidable conclusion that my only daughter had taken it upon herself to be offended by Mr McCorquindale!

**5.**

I naturally entered the chamber forthwith.

Therein I found the tobacco merchant . . . sound asleep.

I observed him for a full two hours – snoring with the abandoned alacrity of the vagrant.

When he finally awoke his face had such a peaceable expression that I deemed it politic to make my point.

'Mr McCorquindale,' says I, 'I believe Mr Buccleuch owes you a hundred guineas.'

'He does,' says he.

'What of it?'

'Would you consider letting him pay it back over a period of time?' says I.

'I would not,' says he.

And the peaceable expression vanished from his face.

'But he wishes to marry my daughter,' says I, 'and he cannot do so if you require immediate repayment.'

'You are once again considering this effeminate romancer as a partner for your only daughter?' says he.

'He stands up for his principles,' says I.

'For which your crew made him *walk the plank*, as they say?'

'It was I that gave the order,' says he.

'Are you not ashamed?' says I.

'An example was required,' says he.

'And for an example you made the boy swim many miles in *shark-infested waters*?'

'The ship,' says he, 'was anchored not three hundred yards from the shore at the time.

Master Buccleuch swam to land in minutes.

The young gentlemen is of an hysterical temperament.

Better suited to stage melodrama than the sea.'

I myself recognised this tendency of Master Buccleuch's.

So I deemed it politic to say nothing further.

## 6.

I broached instead the other matter.

Says I to Mr McCorquindale: 'Did you insult my daughter?'

'And what makes you say that?' says he.

'She claims you invited her to be your live-in housekeeper,' says I, 'which is tantamount in some circles to being your whore.'

'That is not an insult,' says he.

'Your daughter is but a plain-faced ugly girl.

To be the whore of a tobacco merchant would be a feather in any young lady's cap.'

'Mr McCorquindale,' says I, 'I must insist that you withdraw this insult to my daughter.'

'I will do no such thing,' says he.

'It's you that should withdraw your insult to me.'

'Which insult was that?' says I.

'Why the insult,' says he, 'of you accusing me of insulting your daughter.'

'I will not,' says I.

'In that case,' says he, 'you will move out of Virginia Street by the end of the week.

And your major debts will be henceforth reinstated.'

'I will live in the gutter,' says I, 'rather than have my family honour besmirched.'

'By the end of the week,' says he.

'By the end of the week.

By the end of the week.'

And off he goes with his juvenile chanting.

Showing no concern whether or no I had been left in despair.

**7.**

And now the hooligan wants me to go round.

In an hour's time.

Which is almost upon us.

Well, what choice have I got?

Euphemia will no longer be able to marry Master Buccleuch.

And the girl will have to have somewhere to live.

If it was just myself I'd rest content with a hovel.

But I cannot put my only daughter through such purgatory.

There's nothing else for it.

Humble pie will have to be eaten, Dalmellington.

Humble pie will have to be eaten.

Humble pie will have to be eaten.


**8.**

*He puts his coat on.*
*He goes out whistling.*


**Five**

**1.**

*We find* **Dalmellington** *on. He turns to us.*


**2.**

Widow MacKay has just come up.

Euphemia had called round with a goose, a fresh leek and a turnip from her kitchen garden.

My only daughter is now living with her husband and is happy in the knowledge that her father will never be in want.

**3.**

I say Widow MacKay from habit.

But the good lady is a widow no longer.

She is a mistress again.

Mistress Dalmellington, to be precise.

Following a visit of the then Widow MacKay to Grahamston, says I to the good lady: 'Has Mistress Zapata *never* condescended to consult on personal matters?'

'Concerning myself?' says the Widow.

'Concerning thyself *and* myself,' says I.

'Oh Mistress Zapata sees thyself and myself *united*,' says she.

'We are to lose our independence to each other?' says I.

'Yes, but with the common cause of gaining independence *for our nation*,' says she.

'And does Mistress Zapata say anything about whether or not auld Scotia will ever reach such an exalted state?' says I.

'She has never been able to bring up a clear image of an independent Scotland,' says she.

'For the issue is shrouded in mystery centuries into the future.'

**4.**

Unusually crowded Trongate on my way to Mr McCorquindale's.

The tobacco merchants were assembling to hear a public pronouncement.

And flitting in and out among them is Master Buccleuch.

He looked as though sleep and he had not been friends of late.

'It is my abiding hope,' says he, 'that my marriage to your daughter will go ahead.

For which reason I must request a review of your financial situation.'

'Mr McCorquindale has refused to countenance any smoothing the passage of any marriage between yourself and my daughter,' says I.

'Then the hopes of myself and Euphemia are indeed done for,' says he.

'And Mr McCorquindale is an evil man, who does not believe all men are equal.'

'Pray, sir, expand upon your meaning,' says I.

'Well, during the voyage,' says he, 'Mr McCorquindale would get drunk and force himself on the female slaves.

Till three of them became visibly impregnated.'

'I am outraged,' says I.

'The hooligan has failed to read the latest authors on the subject of slavery.'


## 5.

I would have said more but the town crier climbed on to the podium and made his announcement.

We are at war with the American colonies.

To say that a cloud of gloom descended on the assembled tobacco merchants would be an understatement.

When they expressed their fears of lost trade and ruin I nodded sympathetically.

But said nothing of my deepest hope that what is good for the American colonies today might come to pass for auld Scotia tomorrow.

## 6.

You will doubtless wish to know that when I reached McCorquindale's on the aforementioned day I was determined to act on behalf of my daughter and *demand* an apology.

'My humblest apologies,' says he before I had uttered a word, 'for any insult taken by your daughter.'

'My behaviour is entirely a result of my drinking habit.

It was my many lonely years in the American colonies.

I developed a great jealousy of gentlemen such as yourself who had the opportunity to raise offspring from a young age.

And it has always been my intention to find a suitable woman who would have no prejudice against my advanced years.

Accordingly I would ask to take the hand of your Euphemia in marriage.'

My astonishment was so great that I was frozen into silence.

'Euphemia and myself will move into one of the new houses in St Andrew's Square,' he went on.

'Ownership of Virginia Street will revert to yourself, access to the entire house will be reinstated and all your debts eradicated forthwith.'

Says I to Mr McCorquindale: 'An offer of stupendous munificence.

I will – of course – put it to my daughter.

But you must know that – speaking as a mother – it has always been my policy not to impose my will on her.'

'Nonetheless I am certain,' says he, 'that your daughter will be susceptible to your guidance.'

'That may be so, sir, but if I also may have your thoughts regarding the relative status of the black race.'

'Why sir,' says he, 'the black man is generally considered to be an inferior species, closer to the apes.'

'If I may suggest,' says I, 'that you acquaint yourself with the latest authors at your earliest convenience.'

To which plan he committed himself wholeheartedly.

Content that my thorough investigation of the tobacco merchant's moral standing had been satisfactorily concluded I made my way home to inform my daughter of Mr McCorquindale's offer.


## 7.

Whereupon I made it abundantly clear that the answer was *entirely* up to Euphemia.

And the promised substantial improvement in her father's living conditions she was under no obligation to take into account.

At which my only daughter paced up and down.

Turned red in the face.

Emitted a scream.

Short but piercing.

I must confess I was not optimistic.

But then – says my only daughter to me –

'Father darling Father.

*My* happiness can be of no concern but if there is *anything* I may do to secure *your* happiness I will most certainly do it.

I will marry Mr McCorquindale happily.'

'Are you quite sure,' says I, 'that you will be happy in such an arrangement?'

'I will be happy,' says she, 'in any arrangement that makes you happy.'

And speaking as a mother to my daughter I was most happy to take a sympathetic interest in my daughter's sympathetic interest in her father's happiness.

Clearly the torment I had observed in my only daughter was – in fact – joy in the highest.

Indeed I thanked God for the continuing mystery of the female sex!

## 8.

When Mr Buccleuch heard of the upcoming wedding he came to me.

Says he, 'I will appear at St Andrew's Kirk and object to the marriage.'

'On what grounds?' says I.

'Why, on the grounds,' says he, 'that McCorquindale has had children out of wedlock with slave women.'

I did not protest at this outrageous accusation.

For I found it impossible not to sympathise with the boy's youthful jealousy.

Indeed I had a word with Mr McCorquindale about the boy's intentions.

Whereupon the great man most generously made it his business to seek the assistance of his many contacts.

And ensure Mr Buccleuch would be enlisted in the first round of call-ups for the American War, several weeks ahead of the wedding.

Thus providing the boy with the opportunity to fight for his country.

Not wanting to cast a shadow over my daughter's happiest of days I did not warn her of Mr Buccleuch's threatened intervention.

And so it was that the great day passed without mishap or disturbance.

## 9.

Then just last week we heard the sad news that the boy had been . . .

That he had been reported as . . .

It is my opinion the *Herald* was remiss in employing such overblown and sensational phraseology as 'killed in action'.

But it did occur to me that this was a sign that any marriage between Master Buccleuch and my daughter was never meant to be.

I made it my business to go round and regretfully communicate the sad news to my daughter.

But I was shaken off my course by her announcement that she is to be a mother.

Yes I, Enoch Dalmellington, am to be a grandfather.

It is – sad to say – unlikely to be a rich future for my grandson.

Indeed his father has made heavy losses due to the American War.

And his plans for a house in St Andrew's Square have given way to a more modest dwelling.

On the Briggait.

## 10.

The future outlook was not improved by my first visit to Mistress Zapata.

The self-professed political medium claimed that not only will the Glasgow trade in tobacco come to a halt, the city will cease to be a commercial port altogether and the once mighty Clyde will be thronged only by the ghosts of trading vessels past.

And indeed our great river will be lined with towering dwelling houses of shoddy workmanship, unprecedented ugliness and enormous expense.

And that the unfortunate citizens who made such purchases would one day be imprisoned indefinitely in their riverside slums by a catastrophic decline in house values.

It was all I could do to contain my laughter.

The hard-headed citizens of Glasgow could not possibly be duped in such a fashion.

'My dear wife,' says I, 'I must inform you that my first visit to Mistress Zapata's shall also be my last.'


ENDING FOR THEATRES CONVERTED FROM CHURCHES

I bethought me to pursue her on some of her sacrilegious prophecies.

Says I: 'Did you indeed predict that there will be box receptacles in every drawing room in the land?'

'Yes indeed,' says she. 'For in these receptacles mighty epics will appear.

Pride of place being taken by the exploits of such as William Wallace, Rob Roy McGregor and the . . . pirates of the Caribbean.'

'Could I request,' says I, 'that you refrain from equating celebrated heroes with infamous villains?'

Or I would have said had not the medium pressed on with an additional revelation.

That the churches will one day be converted into theatres.

And that the price of a pew for one hour will equal the present tariff for an entire year.

Actors in a theatre is a prospect sufficiently dismal.

But actors in a church?

Never never never, say I.

Never!


ENDING FOR OTHER THEATRES

I bethought me to pursue her on some of her sacrilegious prophecies.

Says I: 'Did you indeed predict that there will be box receptacles in every drawing room in the land?'

'Yes indeed,' says she. 'For in these receptacles mighty epics will appear.

Pride of place being taken by the exploits of such as William Wallace, Rob Roy McGregor and the . . . pirates of the Caribbean.'

'Could I request,' says I, 'that you refrain from equating celebrated heroes with infamous villains?'

Actors in a theatre is a prospect sufficiently dismal.

But actors in the drawing room?

Never never never, say I.

Never!

## Methuen Drama Student Editions

Jean Anouilh *Antigone* • John Arden *Serjeant Musgrave's Dance*
Alan Ayckbourn *Confusions* • Aphra Behn *The Rover* • Edward Bond
*Lear* • *Saved* • Bertolt Brecht *The Caucasian Chalk Circle* • *Fear and
Misery in the Third Reich* • *The Good Person of Szechwan* • *Life of Galileo* •
*Mother Courage and her Children* • *The Resistible Rise of Arturo Ui* • *The
Threepenny Opera* • Anton Chekhov *The Cherry Orchard* • *The Seagull* •
*Three Sisters* • *Uncle Vanya* • Caryl Churchill *Serious Money* • *Top Girls*
• Shelagh Delaney *A Taste of Honey* • Euripides *Elektra* • *Medea* •
Dario Fo *Accidental Death of an Anarchist* • Michael Frayn *Copenhagen*
• John Galsworthy *Strife* • Nikolai Gogol *The Government Inspector* •
Robert Holman *Across Oka* • Henrik Ibsen *A Doll's House* • *Ghosts* •
*Hedda Gabler* • Charlotte Keatley *My Mother Said I Never Should* •
Bernard Kops *Dreams of Anne Frank* • Federico García Lorca *Blood
Wedding* • *Doña Rosita the Spinster* (bilingual edition) • *The House of
Bernarda Alba* • (bilingual edition) • *Yerma* (bilingual edition) • David
Mamet *Glengarry Glen Ross* • *Oleanna* • Patrick Marber *Closer* • John
Marston *Malcontent* • Martin McDonagh *The Lieutenant of Inishmore* •
Joe Orton *Loot* • Luigi Pirandello *Six Characters in Search of an Author*
• Mark Ravenhill *Shopping and F\*\*\*ing* • Willy Russell *Blood Brothers*
• *Educating Rita* • Sophocles *Antigone* • *Oedipus the King* • Wole
Soyinka *Death and the King's Horseman* • Shelagh Stephenson *The
Memory of Water* • August Strindberg *Miss Julie* • J. M. Synge *The
Playboy of the Western World* • Theatre Workshop *Oh What a Lovely
War* Timberlake Wertenbaker *Our Country's Good* • Arnold Wesker
*The Merchant* • Oscar Wilde *The Importance of Being Earnest* •
Tennessee Williams *A Streetcar Named Desire* • *The Glass Menagerie*

# Methuen Drama Modern Plays

*include work by*

Edward Albee
Jean Anouilh
John Arden
Margaretta D'Arcy
Peter Barnes
Sebastian Barry
Brendan Behan
Dermot Bolger
Edward Bond
Bertolt Brecht
Howard Brenton
Anthony Burgess
Simon Burke
Jim Cartwright
Caryl Churchill
Complicite
Noël Coward
Lucinda Coxon
Sarah Daniels
Nick Darke
Nick Dear
Shelagh Delaney
David Edgar
David Eldridge
Dario Fo
Michael Frayn
John Godber
Paul Godfrey
David Greig
John Guare
Peter Handke
David Harrower
Jonathan Harvey
Iain Heggie
Declan Hughes
Terry Johnson
Sarah Kane
Charlotte Keatley
Barrie Keeffe

Howard Korder
Robert Lepage
Doug Lucie
Martin McDonagh
John McGrath
Terrence McNally
David Mamet
Patrick Marber
Arthur Miller
Mtwa, Ngema & Simon
Tom Murphy
Phyllis Nagy
Peter Nichols
Sean O'Brien
Joseph O'Connor
Joe Orton
Louise Page
Joe Penhall
Luigi Pirandello
Stephen Poliakoff
Franca Rame
Mark Ravenhill
Philip Ridley
Reginald Rose
Willy Russell
Jean-Paul Sartre
Sam Shepard
Wole Soyinka
Simon Stephens
Shelagh Stephenson
Peter Straughan
C. P. Taylor
Theatre Workshop
Sue Townsend
Judy Upton
Timberlake Wertenbaker
Roy Williams
Snoo Wilson
Victoria Wood

## Methuen Drama Modern Classics

Jean Anouilh *Antigone* • Brendan Behan *The Hostage* • Robert Bolt
*A Man for All Seasons* • Edward Bond *Saved* • Bertolt Brecht *The
Caucasian Chalk Circle* • *Fear and Misery in the Third Reich* • *The Good
Person of Szechwan* • *Life of Galileo* • *The Messingkauf Dialogues* •
*Mother Courage and Her Children* • *Mr Puntila and His Man Matti* •
*The Resistible Rise of Arturo Ui* • *Rise and Fall of the City of
Mahagonny* • *The Threepenny Opera* • Jim Cartwright *Road* • *Two &
Bed* • Caryl Churchill *Serious Money* • *Top Girls* • Noël Coward
*Blithe Spirit* • *Hay Fever* • *Present Laughter* • *Private Lives* • *The Vortex* •
Shelagh Delaney *A Taste of Honey* • Dario Fo *Accidental Death of an
Anarchist* • Michael Frayn *Copenhagen* • Lorraine Hansberry *A
Raisin in the Sun* • Jonathan Harvey *Beautiful Thing* • David Mamet
*Glengarry Glen Ross* • *Oleanna* • *Speed-the-Plow* • Patrick Marber
*Closer* • *Dealer's Choice* • Arthur Miller *Broken Glass* • Percy Mtwa,
Mbongeni Ngema, Barney Simon *Woza Albert!* • Joe Orton
*Entertaining Mr Sloane* • *Loot* • *What the Butler Saw* • Mark Ravenhill
*Shopping and F\*\*\*ing* • Willy Russell *Blood Brothers* • *Educating Rita* •
*Stags and Hens* • *Our Day Out* • Jean-Paul Sartre *Crime Passionnel* •
Wole Soyinka • *Death and the King's Horseman* • Theatre Workshop
*Oh, What a Lovely War* • Frank Wedekind • *Spring Awakening* •
Timberlake Wertenbaker *Our Country's Good*

For a complete catalogue
of Methuen Drama titles
write to:

Methuen Drama
Bloomsbury Publishing Plc
36 Soho Square
London W1D 3QY

or you can visit our website at
www.methuendrama.com